CLIMATE CHANGE IMPACT
Communities at Risk

Don Nardo

San Diego, CA

About the Author

Classical historian, amateur astronomer, and award-winning author Don Nardo has written numerous volumes about scientific topics, including *Destined for Space* (winner of the Eugene M. Emme Award for best astronomical literature), *Tycho Brahe* (winner of the National Science Teaching Association's best book of the year), *Deadliest Dinosaurs*, and *The History of Science*. Nardo, who also composes and arranges orchestral music, lives with his wife, Christine, in Massachusetts.

© 2025 ReferencePoint Press, Inc.
Printed in the United States

For more information, contact:
ReferencePoint Press, Inc.
PO Box 27779
San Diego, CA 92198
www.ReferencePointPress.com

ALL RIGHTS RESERVED.
No part of this work covered by the copyright hereon may be reproduced or used in any form or by any means—graphic, electronic, or mechanical, including photocopying, recording, taping, web distribution, or information storage retrieval systems—without the written permission of the publisher.

Picture Credits:
Cover: michel lippitsch/Shutterstock.com

6: Alexander Demyanenko/Shutterstock.com
10: Daniel A Varela/TNS/Newscom
13: Felix Mizioznikov/Shutterstock.com
16: Mari_May/Shutterstock.com
20: ZUMA Press, Inc./Alamy Stock Photo
23: USDA Photo/Alamy Stock Photo
26: SM AKBAR ALI PJ/Shutterstock.com

30: David Peinado Romero/Shutterstock.com
33: MD. Rakibul Hasan/Alamy Stock Photo
36: robertharding/Alamy Stock Photo
40: 24K-Production/iStock
43: Alexander Raths/Shutterstock.com
45: Penny Tweedie/Alamy Stock Photo
49: Kayte Deioma/Alamy Stock Photo
51: Frances Roberts/Alamy Stock Photo
53: Watchtheworld/Alamy Stock Photo

LIBRARY OF CONGRESS CATALOGING-IN-PUBLICATION DATA

Names: Nardo, Don, 1947- author.
Title: Climate change impact : communities at risk / by Don Nardo.
Description: San Diego, CA : ReferencePoint Press, [2025] | Series: Climate change impact | Includes bibliographical references and index.
Identifiers: LCCN 2024000175 (print) | LCCN 2024000176 (ebook) | ISBN 9781678208240 (library binding) | ISBN 9781678208257 (ebook)
Subjects: LCSH: Climatic changes--Social aspects--Juvenile literature. | Climatic changes--Effect of human beings on--Juvenile literature.
Classification: LCC QC903 .N3435 2025 (print) | LCC QC903 (ebook) | DDC 363.7--dc23/eng/20240108
LC record available at https://lccn.loc.gov/2024000175
LC ebook record available at https://lccn.loc.gov/2024000176

CONTENTS

Introduction 4
Communities Threatened by a Warming World

Chapter One 8
Destruction Caused by Extreme Weather

Chapter Two 18
Threats to Fresh Water and Food Production

Chapter Three 28
Residents of Communities Displaced

Chapter Four 38
Climate Change's Impact on the Most Vulnerable

Chapter Five 47
Communities Adapting to Climate Change

Source Notes	56
Organizations and Websites	59
For Further Research	60
Index	61

INTRODUCTION

Communities Threatened by a Warming World

"San Francisco's future looks a whole lot wetter, thanks in part to human-caused climate change," says Ezra David Romero, a California reporter who specializes in climate-related phenomena. "San Francisco will be hit by increasingly intense storms in the coming decades, and needs to dramatically update its stormwater infrastructure to try to handle the deluge."[1] Kris May, founder of San Francisco's Pathways Climate Institute, agrees. "We're gonna see more areas that flood that have never flooded before," he states. "I don't think we have nomenclature [descriptive terms] anymore for what is coming with climate change. . . . I don't think any city is really in the shape to prepare for the storms that are coming. It's just going to be a big change that the country as a whole has to deal with."[2]

These and similar remarks by other climate experts came on the heels of a major study released in February 2023 by Moody's Analytics, the widely respected financial firm that does global research on threats to the world's economy. After examining reams of evidence, the Moody's researchers listed the ten US communities that are presently most at risk for severe hazards caused by climate change. San Francisco was first on the list. It was followed by Cape Coral, Florida; New York City; Long Island, New York; and six others. "San Francisco is not especially susceptible to any one hazard," Moody's concluded. "But above-average risk from each category makes it the [country's] single-most exposed large metro area or division."[3]

The Dangers of Rising Warmth

Climate change, along with its hazards, such as more and stronger rainstorms and hurricanes, can be briefly described overall as a steady warming of earth's atmosphere and oceans during the past two centuries. Scientists now have irrefutable proof that the chief causes include the burning of fossil fuels, high-volume agricultural production, and deforestation. These human activities result in the release of carbon dioxide, methane, and other so-called greenhouse gases into the air. The gases form a layer in the atmosphere that, like a greenhouse, traps the sun's heat that otherwise would be reflected off the planet and back into space. Over time, this process will steadily warm the earth's average temperatures.

In turn, the rising warmth increases the number, duration, and intensity of heat waves, droughts, large-scale wildfires, and hurricanes and other ocean storms. Another major effect is rising sea levels and the flooding that often accompanies them. These and other effects of disjointed, extreme weather are already adversely affecting human communities not only in the United States but all over the world.

Moreover, some towns and cities are being hit harder than others. Moody's singled out San Francisco in part because climate scientists estimate the sea level in the city's bay and surrounding waters is likely to rise 3 to 6 feet (91.4 to 182.9 cm) in the coming decades. That is enough to permanently flood a large portion of the city's central section. Other threats to the

CONSIDER THIS

The San Francisco Bay Area, which is presently threatened by climate change, contains one hundred cities and towns and a population of more than 7 million people.

—California Energy Commission

community connected to climate change were listed in California's official 2018 state climate change assessment. In an initial summary, the report warned that in the coming years the city's airports, roads, and railways will likely periodically flood. And the community's electrical grid "is vulnerable to power outages during wind and wildfire events while much of our natural gas transmission system

San Francisco is number one of the ten US cities most at risk for severe hazards caused by climate change. According to experts, the city will be hit by increasingly intense storms in the coming decades.

is located along waterways and will be impacted by flooding from sea level rise and extreme storm events," says the report. "Increasing seawater intrusion into groundwater . . . and levee [dam] failures . . . will affect both the quantity of water available and the quality of supplies."[4]

Climate Change's Creeping Effects

It must be emphasized that the plight of San Francisco and the other US cities most at risk in the decades ahead is far from unique. All around the globe, human communities large and small are threatened by climate change. "We are seeing its creeping effects now," say Allegra Kirkland and other reporters for the popular technology and business website Quartz. Indeed, they say, the increasing effects of climate change are seen "with hurricanes like Maria and Harvey that caused hundreds of deaths and billions of dollars in economic damage; with the Mississippi River and its tributaries overflowing their banks . . . leaving huge swaths of the Midwestern plains under water. Climate change is, at this very moment, taking a real toll on wildlife, ecosystems, economies, and human beings [in numerous communities]."[5]

6

The experts further warn that as time goes on, recovering from various climate change–driven disasters will become much more difficult. In the past, cleaning up and rebuilding after natural disasters was paid for by a combination of insurance companies and state and federal government agencies. But as Moody's points out, that traditional system is already breaking down, which could lead to calamitous circumstances for millions of Americans. The Moody's report warns:

> Rising temperatures mean more frequent and severe natural disasters that could destroy homes and spark out-migration from some areas. Similarly, enough disasters will eventually force insurers to abandon markets they deem too risky; this has already happened in some parts of the country, including much of Florida, forcing [government agencies] to step in. That practice, however, will be difficult to sustain and could eventually compel more people to move out of areas that become classified as uninsurable.[6]

Not surprisingly, climate scientists, concerned community leaders, and a growing number of ordinary citizens would prefer to avoid the most dire predicted effects of the rapidly changing climate. To that end, some steps have already been taken to slow it down or reverse its effects. Alternately, some towns and cities have decided to learn to adapt to climate change. Whichever the approach, there is general agreement that the worst possible outcomes of a warming world are not necessarily inevitable and that more can be done to avoid them, or at least reduce their impact. As Texas Tech University scientist Katharine Hayhoe puts it, "The future is not set in stone"; furthermore, "the amount of change that we're going to see—whether it's serious, whether it's dangerous, whether it's devastating, whether it's civilization-threatening—the amount of change we're going to see is up to us. It depends on our choices today and in the next few years."[7]

CHAPTER ONE

Destruction Caused by Extreme Weather

Under the slow but relentless onslaught of climate change, communities large and small on the US Eastern Seaboard are getting not only warmer and warmer but also wetter and wetter. The same is true of towns and cities in western Europe, Australia, eastern and southern Asia, and central Africa, along with some other global regions. This was the key finding of an important study of earth's changing climate released in mid-2023. Published in the respected scientific journal *Earth's Future*, the study was conducted at China's Northwest A&F University, with world-renowned climate researcher Haijiang Wu as the lead author.

Wu and his colleagues concluded that, although some parts of the world are getting hotter and dryer, or "dry-hot," thanks to climate change, others will become increasingly "wet-hot" in the decades ahead. The principal reason for this form of extreme weather, the researchers explain, is related to the way the planet's atmosphere absorbs water. Scientists have known for more than two centuries that the warmer the air, the more moisture it can absorb. Eventually, enough water builds up in each expanse of air until it is released as precipitation in the form of rain or snow.

The 2023 study points out that climate change is steadily increasing the incidence and intensity of this fundamental physical process. As the atmosphere progressively warms, the air above some areas of the planet is retaining much more moisture than normal. For every rise in temperature of 1.8°F (1°C), the ability of a given volume of air to hold on to water vapor increases by 6 to 7 percent. In turn, that means that over the course of months and years, more water will be available to fall as precipitation on that area.

In the wake of increasing climate change, the excess moisture is causing and will continue to cause various outcomes that are detrimental to human civilization. First, say scientists at the American Geophysical Union in Washington, DC, "When wet-hot conditions strike, heat waves first dry out the soil and reduce its ability to absorb water. Subsequent rainfall then has a harder time penetrating the soil and instead runs along the surface, contributing to flooding, landslides and crop failures."[8]

This scenario is complicated by the fact that the land areas most likely to be affected by wet-hot extremes contain numerous heavily populated communities. The string of dozens of large cities and towns clustered along the American Eastern Seaboard, from Maine to Florida, is a prominent example. That region is already prone to flooding generated by another serious outcome of climate change—sea level rise. Miami and New York City are only two of many seaboard communities that are already struggling with floods caused by rising sea levels.

Moreover, flash floods, landslides, and crop losses are increasing in the eastern United States, western Europe, and elsewhere as by-products of excess water in the air. The large flash floods and massive landslides that struck western Europe in the summer of 2021, claiming more than two hundred lives, constitute only one example. The growing threat to life in such heavily populated areas prompted Wu to remark, "If we overlook the risk of . . . wet-hot extremes and fail to take sufficient early warning, the [negative] impacts . . . would be unimaginable."[9]

> ## CONSIDER THIS
>
> From 2010 to 2022 governments and large companies worldwide spent roughly $600 billion annually to slow climate change. Climate scientists estimate that at least four times that much per year will be needed to do the job.
>
> —*New York Times*

Larger-than-Normal Precipitation Events

It turned out that 2021 witnessed many more destructive flash floods than the ones that wreaked havoc in western Europe. That brand of extreme-weather-driven disaster, a result of climate change, occurred in towns and cities all over the world that year. On August 21 in New York City, for instance, nearly 2 inches (5 cm) of rain fell in Central Park in a single hour, the most the city had ever before experienced in so short a time. Yet incredibly, that record was obliterated a mere eleven days later, when 3.15 inches (8 cm) of rain poured down on the city in the space of an hour.

As a result of these downpours, most of the city's subway tunnels flooded, bringing travel via that vast underground railway system to a halt. Meanwhile, aboveground, the torrential rains triggered still more chaos as numerous streets and underpasses flooded. Thousands of motorists abandoned their cars. At the same time, thousands of other residents, mainly those with basement apartments, lost many of their belongings as water poured from the streets into their homes.

Miami is already struggling with floods caused by rising sea levels. This photo shows flooding in the neighborhood of Little Havana that occurred in June 2022 after heavy rain.

Death in a Chinese Tunnel

The flash floods that struck western Europe and New York City in the summer of 2021 were far from unique. Similar massive precipitation events spawned by climate change happened in other parts of the world in that same period. On July 21, 2021, for example, in Zhengzhou, China, a sudden flash flood trapped hundreds of people in the city's large subway system. Before the floodwaters subsided, twelve people had died.

Some of the survivors took cell phone videos that showed many of the trapped residents urgently struggling to breathe in random pockets of air as the water rapidly rose. After the tragedy, Slobodan Djordjevic, an engineer at England's University of Exeter and a leading expert on the mechanics of subway floods, reviewed the videos and told an NPR reporter, "None of us had seen people with water up to their necks, standing in underground trains." Besides the deaths that occurred, he said, more than five hundred other people would surely have drowned if rescuers had not rushed down into the flooded tunnels to save them. He said that the images on the videos were so graphic and disturbing, "I actually considered whether this was even real."

Quoted in Rebecca Hersher, "NYC's Subway Flooding Isn't a Fluke. It's the Reality for Cities in a Warming World," *All Things Considered*, NPR, September 2, 2021. www.npr.org.

Following this outbreak of extreme weather, scientists pointed out that climate change–induced sea level rise was not the culprit. True, they explained, such rising sea levels do cause flooding in coastal cities and will continue to do so often in the coming decades. But the flash floods of 2021 were the result of abrupt and much-larger-than-normal precipitation events—that is, massive rainstorms. In the case of the New York floods, the storms were unleashed by a combination of warm, moisture-laden air hanging over both the land portions of the Eastern Seaboard and the nearby ocean.

An Onslaught of Monster Hurricanes

Experts say that the huge amounts of excess water hanging above the ocean consisted primarily of the remnants of Hurricane Ida. That enormous storm had struck New Orleans earlier that week (in mid-August 2021), dropping more than 6 inches (15.2 cm) of rain on towns and cities in southern Louisiana. At the time, it was the second-most-destructive hurricane ever to make landfall in that state. When it moved on after a couple of days, it traveled overland toward the northeast and, though weakened, still packed a considerable punch when it reached New York.

That Ida was potent enough to dump torrential rain on communities in a swath from the Gulf Coast all the way up to New York, do $75.3 billion worth of damage, and kill 107 people was not a fluke. Meteorologists and climate scientists point out that it was part of an ongoing pattern of climate change–driven extreme weather that takes the form of very powerful hurricanes. Put simply, the wet-hot pattern of moisture-laden air seen on land in the eastern United States also occurs in the nearby ocean. There the warmer-than-average air combines with warmer-than-average ocean water.

That water gets warmer because much of the extra atmospheric warmth generated by the changing climate is absorbed by the upper layers of the oceans. Science writer Oliver Milman reports that in 2021, the upper 6,560 feet (2,000 m) of the Atlantic Ocean absorbed an "amount of extra energy 145 times greater than the world's entire electricity generation." As a result, that year "saw the hottest ocean temperatures in recorded history, the sixth consecutive year that this record [had] been broken."[10]

That degree of added warmth in the oceans is problematic, scientists point out, because hurricanes are essentially giant heat engines. As water temperatures rise, what starts out as a small tropical storm grows increasingly large. It also becomes potentially more destructive when it comes ashore and passes over the hundreds of towns and cities huddled along the Gulf Coast and Eastern Seaboard.

Moreover, this pattern of progressively more powerful hurricanes is not something that might occur at some hard-to-predict future date; rather, an onslaught of monster hurricanes has already begun to spread ruin through American coastal communities. To name only a few of Ida's recent sibling storms: in 2018 Florence did $24.2 billion worth of damage and killed 54 people;

In 2022 Hurricane Ian caused mass destruction in Florida. Ian caused $112 billion in damages and took 150 lives.

in 2020 Sally did damages of $7.3 billion and killed 4 persons; and in 2022 Ian caused a whopping $112 billion in damages and took 150 lives. The many deaths and enormous costs of rebuilding after hurricanes is troubling, says the Union of Concerned Scientists. Therefore, the group says, "it is essential to do whatever we can to avoid dangerous [atmospheric and ocean] warming and protect coastal communities for ourselves and our children."[11]

Record Heat Waves and Droughts

In addition to the various negative effects generated by the so-called wet-hot climate change pattern, several examples of extreme weather derive from the pattern that scientists often call dry-hot. Areas where dry-hot conditions are common have far fewer lakes, streams, rivers, and other water sources from which to draw moisture than regions where wet-hot conditions prevail. So the dry-hot areas are considerably drier to begin with, and as the air steadily warms, it and the landforms beneath it tend to

Everyone Will Be Impacted by Climate Change

In his 2022 book on climate change, American climate scientist Joseph Romm briefly explains why researchers like himself are so worried about what could happen to human civilization if the problem of climate change is not seriously addressed in the years ahead. Climate change, he states,

> is now an existential [observed and factual] issue for humanity. Serious climate impacts have already been observed on every continent. Far more dangerous climate impacts are inevitable without much stronger action than the world is currently pursuing, as several major [recent] scientific reports concluded. Since everyone's family will be affected by climate change—indeed, they already are—everyone needs to know the basics about it, regardless of their politics. Many of the major decisions that you, your family, and friends will have to make in the coming years and decades will be affected by human-caused climate change. Should you own coastal property? Should you plan retiring in South Florida? . . . What occupations and career paths make the most sense in a globally warmed world, and what should students study? Should climate change affect how you invest for the future?

Joseph Romm, *Climate Change: What Everyone Needs to Know*. New York: Oxford University Press, 2022, pp. xiii–xiv.

remain dry. The communities in large portions of Europe, China, South America, and the western United States feature such arid conditions on a regular basis.

In recent years, climate change has made these places even drier, sparking record-setting heat waves. In the summer of 2023, a vast and severe heat wave descended on the American Southwest, stretching from Texas in the east to Southern California in the west. Hit especially hard was the city of Phoenix, Arizona. For thirty-one consecutive days, that community suffered from temperatures above 110°F (43°C), smashing the previous record of eighteen straight days set in 1974. At least twenty-five people died in Phoenix of heat-related symptoms in the space of a few weeks. Moreover, the American Southwest was not alone. Similar record-breaking heat waves baked towns and cities in Mexico, southern Europe, China, India, Thailand, and Laos that summer.

Even when temperatures in arid regions rarely go above 100°F (37°C), ongoing climate change frequently keeps average temperatures abnormally high for months or even years at a time. The result is prolonged drought. One of the most insidious and harmful kinds of extreme weather, droughts cause farmers' fields to dry out, killing crops and in poorer communities leading to large-scale starvation. This has been the case in north-central Africa, site of one of the most devastating droughts in modern history. In the 1960s Lake Chad was the world's sixth-largest lake at 10,860 square miles (28,127 sq. km) and a source of irrigation for nearby communities in Cameroon, Chad, Niger, and Nigeria. Today 96 percent of the lake has completely disappeared, in part because temperatures there are rising one and a half times faster than the global average. Tens of thousands of people in the region have died, and in 2023 more than 3 million were food insecure (meaning they didn't always have enough food).

Meanwhile, richer nations are not immune to destructive droughts. In the 2020s numerous communities in the western sector of the United States were still amid a climate change–driven megadrought that began in 2000. The region has seen the depletion of lakes, wells, and community reservoirs, triggering severe water shortages. A study published in 2022 in the respected journal *Nature Climate Change* found that the region has experienced its driest twenty-two-year period since 800 CE, some twelve centuries ago.

> ## CONSIDER THIS
>
> During the huge heat wave in the western United States in the summer of 2023, the temperature in California's Death Valley reached 125.6°F (52°C), one of the highest temperatures ever recorded on earth.
>
> —National Weather Service

Fires of Immense Size and Intensity

The prolonged incidences of heat waves and droughts in the communities featuring dry-hot conditions have also been fueling wildfires of unprecedented number, size, and intensity. The American

West, central Canada, Russian Siberia, and Australia are among the most affected by this sort of climate change–driven activity. Forestry experts report that in several of the US western states, for example, between the mid-1970s and 2023, fire seasons—periods in which wildfires are most likely to occur—increased on average from five to seven months. Many of these fire events were so large in scope that they took months to contain and destroyed substantial portions of communities situated near, and sometimes partially within, major forests.

The main cause of these gigantic blazes also constitutes the key connection between them and the steadily warming climate. The Center for Climate and Energy Solutions, a widely respected environmental policy group, explains that the numerous climate change–driven heat waves and droughts in recent decades have made organic matter in forests (trees, bushes, and dead plants) increasingly dry. And those dried-out materials have gradually accumulated, creating an immense reservoir of burnable material. The latter allows fires that start out small and would normally burn themselves out quickly to gain both in size and intensity.

Australia has been greatly affected by heat waves and droughts that have fueled an unprecedented number of wildfires in recent years. These fires spread out of control and can take weeks to contain.

In recent years examples of the dangers of these catastrophes to human communities have abounded in the heavily forested regions of the western United States and central Canada. In 2020 California endured five of the six largest US wildfires of the modern era. In 2021 the National Interagency Fire Center reported an unprecedented 58,985 wildfires in the United States had burned 7.1 million acres (2.9 million ha) of woodlands. And 2022 witnessed an astounding 68,988 US wildfires, which destroyed 7.6 million acres (3.1 million ha) of forest. Meanwhile, in the first half of 2023, Canada experienced a disturbing 705 percent increase in the number of its wildfires.

> ## CONSIDER THIS
>
> According to several studies conducted by climate experts, the number of Americans who lived within 3 miles (4.8 km) of a large-scale wildfire more than doubled from 2000 to 2023.
>
> —CBS News

Whether enormous wildfires, severe heat waves and droughts, destructive flash floods and landslides, or other manifestations of extreme weather, the connection of these events to climate change becomes clearer, say scientists Daniel Bedford and John Cook. "Each new weather extreme," they write, "adds a new data point to the emerging pattern, and it's the pattern, more than the individual event, that tells the story of a changing climate."[12]

Kevin Trenberth of the National Center for Atmospheric Research in Boulder, Colorado, agrees. In the face of a mountain of undeniable evidence, he says, no one should ask whether a specific event was caused by climate change. Rather, he points out, all of today's extreme weather events are affected to one degree or another by climate change. Therefore, when an example of extreme weather strikes a community, Trenberth says the key question to ask is, "How much did climate change contribute?"[13]

CHAPTER TWO

Threats to Fresh Water and Food Production

The 2020s opened with a terrible spate of water shortages and famines in eastern Africa, where the handful of nations in that region make up that continent's so-called Horn. Millions of the residents of Ethiopia, South Sudan, and Somalia were—and remain—food insecure. And clean fresh water is as scarce in large parts of those lands as nutritious food. Describing the water and food crisis in Somalia, James Elder of the United Nations Children's Fund warned in late 2022, "Without greater action and investment, we are facing the death of children on a scale not seen in half a century."[14]

Elder singled out children because, of the region's overall population, they are most at risk from a health standpoint. In August 2022 alone, he says, roughly forty-four thousand Somalian children were admitted to the country's few functioning medical clinics. All those young people had symptoms of acute malnutrition. That, according to Elder, made them eleven times more likely to die from diarrhea or measles than children in wealthier countries.

What makes the dire situation in Somalia and other sectors of eastern Africa particularly vexing, Elder and other expert observers point out, is that it has multiple causes, all of them complex. Large portions of the area have long suffered from diverse factors that have made farming there difficult. Even before the world entered the industrial age, large ocean storms commonly struck the region, and heat waves, droughts, large-scale floods, and infestations of locusts were far more common there than in other parts of Africa. Moreover, in modern times political and military conflicts have rocked the region. In South Sudan, for example, fighting among rival local factions has led some groups to purposely deny their enemies access to water and food to get the upper hand.

Complicating and greatly amplifying all these problems is the ongoing specter of climate change. A major study released in April 2023 by the World Weather Attribution, made up of a team of international scientists, closely examined the effects of the warming planetary climate on eastern Africa. The group found that as the atmosphere and waters of the western Pacific Ocean grow warmer, complex weather patterns are set in motion that make the trade winds that reach the Horn of Africa extremely dry. As a result, the researchers announced, the towns of eastern Africa are now around one hundred times more likely to experience long, severe droughts than they were before the industrial age set in motion the rapid pace of climate change.

For the communities of the region, the biggest drawback of these perpetual dry spells is that fresh water and food are increasingly hard to come by. In the words of Gernot Laganda of the United Nation's (UN) World Food Programme, in the wake of climate change in eastern Africa, "Natural resources such as clean water and fertile land are becoming scarce, and competition over these resources is becoming fiercer. This is leading to a toxic interplay between the climate crisis, conflict, and hunger."[15]

From Droughts to Contamination

At first glance, for many Americans the water and food shortages in eastern Africa seem far away and a bit hard to imagine. This is because people in most US communities take for granted that ample food and clean water are readily available. Furthermore, in the United States and other well-off countries, there is a general assumption that such availability will always exist.

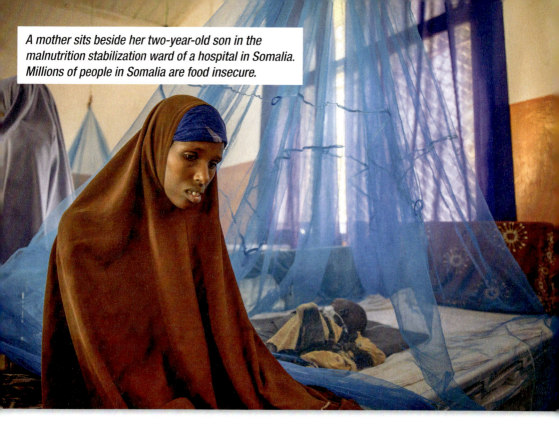

A mother sits beside her two-year-old son in the malnutrition stabilization ward of a hospital in Somalia. Millions of people in Somalia are food insecure.

Yet the reality is very different. American, European, and UN-sponsored climate scientists alike point out that climate change has already negatively impacted US water and food resources. Examining supplies of fresh water first, evidence shows clearly that large numbers of US water sources are already at serious risk. In part this is the result of the increasingly devastating drought conditions affecting communities in the nation's western states. Since early 2020, large portions of Arizona, California, and neighboring states have been enduring the most severe rainfall scarcity of the past twelve centuries. Triggering this drought have been heat waves with near-record-high temperatures and record-low precipitation.

Making matters worse for some communities is the substandard quality of some of the water resources that are still potentially usable. For

CONSIDER THIS

Thanks to climate change–driven droughts, about half of Somalia's citizens—close to 8 million people—were food insecure or close to it in 2022.

—International Rescue Committee

example, the many large-scale wildfires caused by the ongoing drought conditions in the American West cause the soil on forest floors to lose their ability to absorb water. As a result, when rain does fall, it flows away as runoff; and some of it eventually makes its way to streams, rivers, ponds, and lakes. The problem is that the runoff often carries debris and various pollutants created by the unusually high temperatures within the fires. Those substances then proceed to contaminate the lakes and other water sources that local communities employ as reservoirs for drinking water.

The Onset of Saltwater Intrusions

Further complicating the contamination of clean water that communities rely on is the intrusion of salty seawater. Especially prone to such contamination are wells, aquifers, and other underground water sources. Such intrusions were rare before the effects of

The Dangers of Groundwater Drought

As climate change causes various lakes, rivers, community reservoirs, and other kinds of water sources on earth's surface to dry up, water for drinking, bathing, and crop irrigation is growing scarcer in some areas. As a result, many communities around the world are turning to underground water supplies, including wells and aquifers. One often cited example is in farming communities in central and Northern California, the breadbasket region that produces a large portion of North America's vegetables and fruits. "Consider the curious, contested odyssey of the water that fed [those crops]," says NPR agriculture reporter Dan Charles. Most likely, he points out, farmers got that water from underground aquifers. The problem, he explains, is that this process is occurring "on a scale that's become unsustainable, especially as the planet heats up. Facing an ongoing drought that is squeezing surface water supplies, farmers are extracting groundwater at higher rates to continue growing food as usual." This overuse of belowground water sources can lead to what scientists call "groundwater drought," a serious depletion of precious fresh water supplies. Another problem is that when the aquifers are empty, they sometimes cave in, causing damage to underground pipes, roads, and houses.

Dan Charles, "Without Enough Water to Go Around, Farmers in California Are Exhausting Aquifers," *All Things Considered*, NPR, 2021. www.npr.org.

climate change became noticeable in the last decades of the twentieth century. The main cause, scientists say, is the gradual sea level rise caused by melting glaciers and the warming of the oceans. The resulting expansion of the seawater along the coasts allows it to force its way into river deltas and nearby underground pockets of fresh water.

Since the 1990s, small-scale examples of saltwater intrusion have progressively appeared around the country, mostly along the Atlantic and Pacific coasts. Of note have been numerous such events in various locations in Florida. But by far the biggest example the nation has seen to date occurred in late 2023 in Louisiana, where the Mississippi River empties into the Gulf of Mexico. According to researchers at the Tulane University School of Public Health & Tropical Medicine, "Heavier saltwater from the Gulf is moving upriver and displacing freshwater moving downstream because of the lack of rainfall in the Midwest. . . . This lack of rainfall results in a river flow simply not powerful enough and deep enough to prevent the denser saltwater from moving inland and upriver."[16]

Hoping to halt this massive intrusion into the nation's largest freshwater river system, the US Army Corps of Engineers is creating an underwater barrier upstream from the Mississippi Delta. Even if that works, climate scientists say its effects will likely be temporary. That is because climate change–driven sea level rise will keep happening in the decades ahead, and as a result large-scale saltwater intrusions will continue to make headway in the Mississippi and other rivers. In the meantime, the intruding salt water will corrode thousands of water pipes in New Orleans and other communities situated along the rivers, necessitating costly repairs.

Crop Shortages and Food Insecurity

Whether water supplies evaporate in droughts or become polluted by contaminated runoff from wildfires or saltwater intrusion, the resulting lack of fresh water can lead to droughts. And droughts often cause crop losses in some areas. When local agriculture is

This image shows corn crops in Texas that have been devastated by drought. Droughts cause major crop losses in some areas.

disrupted that way, major food shortages can result, and that can lead to widespread food insecurity.

In the most severe cases, famine can occur, as has been happening in large parts of eastern Africa since 2020. In Somalia, for example, agriculture has been the main basis of the economy for centuries. Traditionally, before climate change became a threat, local farming communities grew corn, beans, rice, sugarcane, bananas, and various vegetables. In addition, these communities heavily supplemented the income from those crops by raising goats, sheep, camels, and cattle.

In the wake of climate change–driven droughts in 2020 and beyond, however, many Somali communities suffered major crop losses. The severe reduction in rain-fed foodstuffs also made it increasingly difficult to feed the animals, so the market for livestock suffered near total collapse. Before the onset of the droughts, for example, local farmer and herder Hawa Hassan owned more than six hundred goats. But with almost no water or food to sustain them, less than two years later they numbered only thirty-five. "This is our only source of income," she told an American journalist in 2022. "If our animals die, we might be next. There is no way for us humans to stay alive without them."[17]

By the end of 2022, the Somali government's minister of health estimated that the ongoing dearth of water and food had directly killed some forty-three thousand Somalis in that year alone. Often, he said, people become so weak that they cannot fight off illnesses such as diarrhea and measles. Furthermore, sheer desperation is causing social disorder, say officials at the International Rescue Committee, an organization that tries to help communities in crisis. "People are forced to make impossible choices," they point out. "For example, they are having to . . . marry off children, or sell their own bodies in order to get enough money to survive."[18]

Too Much Water

The array of droughts and food shortages in regions like eastern Africa, where dry-hot weather is the norm, constitutes one of the two main ways that climate change affects farming communities and food production. The other way consists of the effects of climate change on such communities in areas where wet-hot weather conditions prevail. These areas typically receive too much, rather than too little, rain.

As climate change continues to worsen year by year, farmers in villages and towns in wet-hot regions are frequently plagued by an array of difficulties. One, for instance, is that the extra moisture promotes the expansion of weeds that tend to choke out edible crops. Those same regions frequently witness increased attacks on crops by insects and plant diseases, soil erosion, and heavy runoff of excess precipitation. Such runoff carries nutrients and fertilizers away from farmers' fields.

> ### CONSIDER THIS
>
> During the early 2020s, rainfall in Africa increased by some 30 percent in wetter areas and decreased by about 20 percent in drier areas.
>
> —US Embassy and Consulates in Italy

Climate Change Delivers a Double Whammy

Not surprisingly, the "dry-hot" vs. "wet-hot" weather scenarios—which are often intensified by climate change—are felt in more ways than the amount of rain that falls on certain regions. These conditions also affect food security in those places. Coupled with rising atmospheric temperatures, both a lack of rain and too much rain can badly damage food production. Most often, a given geographic area suffers exclusively from the effects of either too little or too much moisture. However, on occasion, both scenarios can strike one region in rapid succession, generating widespread food shortages. This happened in Nigeria, in west-central Africa, in 2021 and 2022. First, in the summer and fall of 2021, there was a long delay in normal rainfall patterns, resulting in a drought. Local authorities estimated a crippling 65 percent reduction in crop harvests. The rains did come, rather suddenly, in the summer of 2022. But they struck with enormous force and dumped more water on the country than it normally receives in multiple seasons. In turn, this caused major floods. Almost all the crops that had managed to survive the earlier drought were destroyed, 612 people were killed, and more than 1.5 million Nigerians were driven from their homes.

Still another problem associated with food production in wet-hot conditions is particularly prevalent in coastal regions of poor and rich countries alike. Namely, many farming communities situated on or near coastlines are increasingly exposed to bigger, stronger ocean storms as well as larger amounts of ordinary rainfall. All that extra water frequently causes widespread erosion and flooding of farmland.

In the United States, one such region is California's San Joaquin Valley, sandwiched between the Pacific Coast and the Sierra Nevada. Since the early 2000s, climate change has made that major food-producing area gradually wetter. That trend continued in early 2023 when torrential rains spawned floods across the valley. Officials in the dairy industry there, which normally generates some $7 billion in revenue annually, estimated that the floods caused losses of at least $20 billion.

Although such losses are devastating, affected communities in wealthy nations like the United States have at least the potential

People in Sylhet, Bangladesh, move to a safer place after heavy flooding in 2022. Rising seas are a growing threat in Bangladesh.

to recover over time. In contrast, similar damages to food production in poverty-stricken countries can lead to widespread death and the permanent ruin of farming communities. In Bangladesh, lying northeast of India, for example, close to half of the 170 million residents have an ancestral tie to agriculture. These farmers have traditionally grown large amounts of rice, mangoes, potatoes, and tea. In recent decades, however, climate change has made the ocean storms that used to occasionally strike that country both more numerous and more severe. In addition, sea level rise has made doz-

CONSIDER THIS

Cyclone Sitrang, a large ocean storm that struck Bangladesh in late October 2022, killed twenty-four people, destroyed ten thousand homes, and left over 1 million people homeless.

—The *Guardian*, a global news organization

ens of Bangladeshi farming communities literally disappear from the map. According to the Climate Reality Project, an international group dedicated to fighting climate change, "Rising seas are a growing threat to people all around Bangladesh. . . . By 2050, one in every seven people in Bangladesh will be displaced by climate change [and] with a projected 19.6 inch (50 cm) rise in sea level, [that nation] may lose approximately 11 percent of its land."[19]

Investing in Food Security

World leaders are aware that poorer countries like Bangladesh and Somalia lack the money to effectively counter climate change's damage to food and water resources. Therefore, richer nations are assuming the lion's share of that financial responsibility. In 2022 US president Joe Biden proposed that his country invest billions of dollars in helping nations around the world attain "durable agricultural production."[20] US secretary of state Antony Blinken summed up the overall goal, saying that humanity's ultimate well-being "depends on the food security that we build together."[21]

CHAPTER THREE

Residents of Communities Displaced

Before the more severe effects of climate change began to be felt in Guatemala in the early 2000s, its people could largely feed themselves on a regular basis. Tucked between Honduras in the east and Mexico in the north and west, their nation sported lush, green landscapes that produced bumper crop harvests in most years. The slopes of Guatemala's many mountains were covered with coffee plantations, and farmers raised bananas, corn, sugarcane, and berries in abundance. Many of these foodstuffs reached foreign markets, including Mexico and the United States.

A Guatemalan farmer named Jorge remembered those good times from his childhood in the 1990s. He helped his father grow corn until starting his own farm in the decade that followed. Jorge subsequently got married, and he and his wife had three children. He assumed that agriculture, which employed fully half the country's residents, would continue to sustain his family and his children's families in the future.

But this assumption proved wrong. In the years that followed, Guatemala's weather patterns grew progressively more unstable. Heat waves and droughts became increasingly severe in some regions, while in others far too much rain fell during the wrong times of the year. Such extremes repeatedly ruined harvests of many of the staple crops, rapidly sending millions of farmers and their children into poverty. By 2019 to 2021, farms across the country struggled to make ends meet, and according to an estimate by the World Bank, close to 1 million Guatemalan children suffered from chronic malnutrition.

Jorge and his family found themselves amid this seemingly nightmarish situation, which they learned had been caused mainly by climate change. According to environmental researcher and reporter Abrahm Lustgarten, Jorge's corn crops failed five years in a row, and he came to realize that "he had to get out of Guatemala. The land was turning against him [and he] knew then that if he didn't get out . . . his family might die."[22]

Jorge and his family therefore packed a few necessities and headed north into Mexico. It is unknown whether they planned to try to settle there or to press on and attempt to reach the United States. Friends and relatives later said that Jorge's ultimate destination was uncertain. He and his family seemed to disappear into the growing stream of Central American climate migrants, often also called climate refugees, heading northward in search of better lives.

The Guatemalan climate migrants, whose numbers grow each year, are not alone in their plight. Each year similar groups of desperate people from Honduras and other Central American lands travel northward toward uncertain futures. And thanks to the "relentless confluence of drought, flood, bankruptcy and starvation" wrought by climate change, Lustgarten points out, numerous people around the globe are "facing the same excruciating decision that confronted Jorge."[23]

Dire Atmospheric Predictions

Experts on human migration and immigration confirm that each year more and more people worldwide face that life-altering decision and choose to become climate refugees. By 2023 there were

> **CONSIDER THIS**
>
> By 2050, climate experts predict, at least 143 million people in sub-Saharan Africa, South Asia, and Latin America will be displaced by climate change within their own countries.
>
> —2021 White House report on climate change migration

Guatemalan migrants cross the Rio Grande River, which runs between Mexico and the United States. Guatemala has many climate migrants every year, who seek refuge in the United States and elsewhere.

an alarming 117 million of them. And according to the Institute for Economics and Peace, based in Sydney, Australia, by 2050 their number will likely reach 1.2 billion—a staggering one-eighth of the planetary population projected for that year.

It is only natural to ask why this large-scale societal and demographic calamity is happening and will only get worse in the years ahead. Part of the answer appeared in a detailed study of the global climate published in 2023 in the widely respected *Proceedings of the National Academy of Sciences*. The researchers entered hundreds of billions of data points about the earth's climate and weather into supercomputers. That allowed the researchers to predict with a fair amount of accuracy how average temperatures around the world will change in the decades ahead and why increasing numbers of people will react by migrating.

One key result of this study consisted of dire projections concerning the planet's atmosphere. Namely, it will undergo a bigger temperature increase in the fifty years from 2023 to 2073 than it did in the past six thousand years combined. That temperature increase will cause geographic areas that are now moderately dry to become deserts. More specifically, the study showed, by 2073 deserts as arid and forbidding as North Africa's infamous Sahara, which today cover only 1 percent of the earth's land surface, will cover almost 20 percent of it.

A Growing Political Issue

Faced with such enormous and frightening changes, a few residents of such regions will choose to stick it out and adapt to the altered conditions. But far more of those locals will choose to migrate to more hospitable areas, climate experts say. And most appealing of all, at least to climate refugees in the Western Hemisphere, is and will continue to be the United States. Mostly this is because of its long-standing reputation as a beacon of democracy, financial opportunities, and equal treatment under the law.

Closely Monitoring the Climate Migrants

Partly because the onrush of climate refugees and other migrants is a controversial issue in American politics, the federal government closely monitors the situation at the southern border. The White House issued one of its periodic studies of the problem in October 2021, saying in part:

> Tens of millions of people [are] likely to be displaced over the next two to three decades due in large measure to climate change impacts. Migration in response to climate impacts may range from mobility as a proactive adaptation strategy to forced displacement in the face of life-threatening risks. This mobility may occur within or across international borders. . . . Migration may be temporary, seasonal, circular, or permanent and may be forced by increasingly severe conditions or occur as a proactive strategy in the face of climate impacts to livelihoods and wellbeing.

> Other wealthy countries, including the United Kingdom, Canada, Germany, and Australia, also regularly study and seek solutions to the climate migration problem. And so does the United Nations, which concerns itself with the needs and problems of all countries.

Whtie House, "Report on the Impact of Climate Change on Migration," October 1, 2021. www.whitehouse.gov.

America's allure in this respect can be seen in the large number of migrants who have recently arrived at its southern border, hoping to gain asylum. In 2022 alone, more than 2 million people arrived at the border. Of those, about 541,000 were from the cluster of nations lying just south of Mexico—Guatemala, Honduras, and San Salvador. Many others came from South America and various Caribbean islands.

It is important to point out that climate change was not the only motivating factor for all of them. Some were fleeing gang violence and political repression in the cities of their home countries. But by far these refugees largely consisted of poor folk—primarily former agricultural workers. Nearly all of them had been displaced by serious climatic changes, including droughts, floods, storms, and the loss of livelihoods brought about by such events.

US leaders have closely monitored the influx of climate refugees in large part because it has become a growing and controversial political issue. Some American politicians do not want any immigrants in the country and seek to block their entry by purposefully sowing confusion about migrants' rights under the law. The American Civil Liberties Union briefly explains those rights, saying that "under U.S. law, a person seeking asylum may do so by arriving at the border and asking to be screened by U.S. officials at a 'port of entry.' . . . [Such asylum seekers] are subjected to a criminal background and security check. They must then navigate a complex and lengthy [legal] process. . . . Those who lose their cases and any appeals . . . are deported."[24]

The number of migrants, a hefty proportion of them climate refugees, who reach the US southern border varies from year to year. So does the number who become US citizens and the number ultimately sent back to their home countries. In 2022 almost

CONSIDER THIS

In 2022 the US government gave the Quinault Indian Nation in Washington State $25 million to help relocate its people as sea level rise claims their traditional lands.

—*New York Times*

2.4 million migrants arrived at the border. More than 1 million of them were soon deported, either because they illegally crossed over the border or because they were ineligible for asylum. The rest were interviewed and allowed to make their cases for asylum in court. Based on numbers from recent years, after the lengthy application process, approximately half of those who apply will likely end up being accepted as US citizens.

Population Displacement in Southeast Asia

In contrast to the climate refugees from Central America, South America, and the Caribbean Islands, most climate migrants from nations on the other side of the globe do not try to reach the United States. This is largely because of the great distances involved. Hence, many of the climate migrants in those lands tend to aim for asylum in countries in their own hemisphere.

Prime examples are the communities in the nations of Southeast Asia, the large, populous area lying south of China, east of India, and west of Australia. During 2017 to 2022, the World Bank

People in Bangladesh live in a temporary shelter after being displaced from their homes by flooding. In Southeast Asia, millions of people have been displaced from their homes because of climate change–related events.

conducted several studies of climate migration generated in those countries. By 2023, the studies found, some 8.5 million residents of the region had already been displaced from their home communities. And an estimated 17 million more will likely be similarly uprooted in the following decade.

The main reason for these predicted migrations is a lack of adequate food to sustain local communities. In fact, the World Bank's studies showed, the Southeast Asian nations will have the highest incidence of food insecurity in the world by the early 2030s. Another important finding was that this adverse situation has and will continue to be driven by a combination of factors. Among them are rapidly rising food prices, financial setbacks caused by the COVID-19 pandemic, and regional military conflicts.

Making all these problems worse, the studies showed, has been a confluence of climate change–induced effects, including droughts, floods, and steadily rising sea levels along those countries' coasts. Recent projections by climate scientists indicate that

Saving Americans from Becoming Climate Refugees

Around the world each year, a great many people are displaced by climate change within their own countries. Indeed, that life-altering process is presently primed to occur in the United States. There, three separate Native American communities are threatened with imminent destruction by rising sea levels. One of them is the village of Newtok in southwest Alaska. It lies below sea level, and melting permafrost is eroding the community's land. Napakiak, a small town located on the shore of Alaska's Kuskokwim River, is also losing 25 to 50 feet (7.6 to 15.2 m) of land annually to erosion as the rising ocean widens the river. The third community, Taholah, home of the Quinault Indian Nation, is situated on Washington State's Olympic Peninsula. It resides in a tsunami zone, and these waters along with rising sea levels are expected to swamp the area. By 2030 climatologists believe these communities will be flooded out of existence and their residents will become climate refugees. To forestall that unwanted outcome, President Joe Biden's administration allotted $75 million in 2022 to cover the costs of relocating the residents of these communities to nearby but safer higher ground.

tens of thousands of square miles of Southeast Asia will be permanently subsumed by the sea by 2050. By then, the experts say, large portions of Vietnam will likely disappear beneath the waves, as will smaller parts of Thailand and Bangladesh.

Up until 2023–2024, the Southeast Asian climate refugees displaced by these varied factors have tended to react in two general ways. One approach has been to leave their home countries and try to settle in other nations. Most of those who have taken that route have ended up in northern India or Middle Eastern countries.

The rest of those Southeast Asians who have been displaced by climate factors lack the resources required for them to make it to foreign lands. Instead, they tend to move from place to place within their own countries. Most often, farmers who suffer from crop failures migrate to the nearest large cities and expand the poorest neighborhoods. In those sprawling urban areas, environmental journalist Abrahm Lustgarten writes, "the most severe strains on society will unfold. [There, most] food has to be imported . . . and people will congregate in slums, with little water or electricity, where they are more vulnerable to flooding or other disasters. The slums fuel extremism and chaos."[25]

> ## CONSIDER THIS
>
> In July 2021 severe floods struck communities in Germany, Belgium, Netherlands, and Luxembourg, killing more than two hundred people and turning thousands more into climate refugees.
>
> —Environmental Justice Foundation

Facing Utter Annihilation

While the destructive effects of climate change in the future will continue to drive some Southeast Asian and other migrants to relocate within their own country's borders, many of those nations will remain physically intact because they are situated on sturdy continental masses that are vulnerable to sea level rise only along their coastlines. In contrast, the rising seas are far more threatening to tiny island nations in the Pacific Ocean, some of which face

35

utter annihilation in the decades ahead. Particularly dire is the plight of Kiribati, a former British colony made up of thirty-three tiny Pacific isles. In recent years the roughly 120,000 residents of that small nation have watched with mounting concern as the ocean waters gradually creep upward, swallowing their communities. Much worse is yet to come, as multiple climate studies indicate that Kiribati will completely disappear beneath the waves sometime between 2050 and 2060.

Hoping to save their homeland, in recent years the Kiribatis have proposed several possible rescue plans. One is to construct high walls on the coasts to keep the seawater out; another was to erect a gigantic floating platform on which people would live and work. Still another proposal was to use giant dredging machines to pick up materials from the nearby seabed. These would be laid directly on the islands in the hope of raising their surfaces high enough to avert disaster.

This is an aerial picture of Tarawa, Kiribati. The islands of this nation are gradually disappearing into the sea and are predicted to vanish completely between 2050 and 2060.

Engineers and financial institutions worldwide have examined these proposals. The general opinion is that even if some are theoretically possible, all will be far too costly for a tiny country like Kiribati to afford. Many experts therefore foresee that the Kiribatis may eventually have no other choice but to evacuate their doomed nation and become climate refugees.

A Need to Act Quickly and Firmly

Whatever Kiribati's fate may be, one thing is certain, says Lustgarten. The growing problem of climate migration will get much worse soon unless the governments of major nations act quickly and firmly. If the richer countries address climate change and climate migration aggressively, he argues, "food production will be shored up, poverty reduced, and international migration slowed. [But] if leaders take fewer actions against climate change, or more punitive ones against migrants, food insecurity will deepen, as will poverty [and] suffering. Whatever actions governments take next, and when they do it, makes a difference."[26]

CHAPTER FOUR

Climate Change's Impact on the Most Vulnerable

"Every single medical device I rely on for survival is either directly powered by electricity or runs on internal batteries that need to be recharged daily,"[27] says Rachel Schmucker, age thirty-eight, of Chambersburg, Pennsylvania. Schmucker has muscular dystrophy, which hampers the contraction of her skeletal muscles and causes her to feel weak, which makes it difficult for her to walk, get dressed, bathe, and sometimes even breathe. She uses an electric wheelchair full time and requires personal care services for most of her daily activities.

Some people may wonder why and how climate change directly affects Schmucker's life. Yet it is something she fears. She states that one of her greatest worries, one she shares with many other individuals with disabilities, is the occurrence of extreme weather events in or near her community. Powerful windstorms, cloudbursts that dump inches of rain at a time, and other severe weather events are major threats to her life and well-being, she explains. That is because they can cause sudden power outages. And all are made more common and more intense by climate change. Thus, she continues, "threats of flash flooding are terrifying because any amount of water would immediately destroy all of this equipment, which costs tens of thousands of dollars per device, and power outages would render them either useless or in danger of draining the batteries until a suitable power source to rechange them is found."[28]

Excess wind and rain and the flooding and power outages they often generate are not the only aspects of climate change that can adversely affect people with disabilities. Heat waves, which are growing worse each year in some communities around the world, constitute another. According to the US Environmental Protection Agency (EPA), "Some people with disabilities are especially at risk for heat-related illness and death. These include individuals with mental health issues, those who depend on others for assistance in daily living, and those with limited mobility or access to transportation. . . . [Such individuals] may not be able to afford air conditioning in their home during heat waves, increasing their risk of heat stroke."[29]

Another potential climate change–related hazard that can directly affect those with disabilities is the sudden onset of an emergency. When a community is imminently threatened by a huge wildfire blazing out of control or a river overthrowing its banks, most residents have a chance to quickly hop in their cars and flee. By contrast, people with disabilities frequently cannot evacuate fast enough, if at all, which puts them more at risk of injury or death.

> ## CONSIDER THIS
>
> In the week ending July 22, 2023, the rate of heat-related hospitalizations in Arizona, California, and Nevada was 51 percent above average.
>
> —Centers for Disease Control and Prevention

Climate Change and a Community's Poorest

The potential negative effects of climate change on various people with disabilities is only one of many examples of what is often referred to as climate equity (sometimes called climate inequity). It is largely a socioeconomic phenomenon in which some people in a community suffer more from climate change's onslaught than others. The social sectors in question tend to be the ones with the highest exposure to risks and hazards and the fewest personal

A woman in a wheelchair is helped into a van. Many people with disabilities rely on equipment like electric wheelchairs that could be rendered useless in the event of a power outage caused by a climate change–related event, like a flash flood.

resources with which to avoid those threats. That makes them society's most vulnerable groups.

Perhaps the largest of those groups, and arguably the most often adversely affected by the ravages of climate change, consists of the poorest individuals in a community. The world's ongoing climate crisis is "a deeply unfair one," a spokesperson for the World Economic Forum points out. This is because poor people, as well as poorer nations, are disproportionately affected by climate change.

> The countries with the fewest resources are likely to bear the greatest burden in terms of loss of life and relative effect on investment and the economy. . . . Only one-tenth of the world's greenhouse gases are emitted by [the] 74 lowest income countries, but they will be most affected by the effects of climate change. [Indeed] they have already experienced approximately eight times as many natural disasters [as richer nations have] in the past 10 years.[30]

Typical of those poorer countries with high rates of poverty is Bangladesh. There, at least 20 percent of the people live below the national poverty line. And twice as many live not far above it. In the United States, by comparison, 12 percent of the population lives below the poverty line.

As a result of the frequent climate change–driven storms and flooding in Bangladesh, each year many impoverished residents lose their homes. "I remember how our house went completely under water," recalls Bangladeshi Bibi Salma. "The river was ferocious," she says, recalling the devastating floods that swept the country's rural southern region in 2020. "It gradually devoured all our farmland and came near our house one day. [Eventually] our orchards, homestead—nothing was left."[31]

Some of the Bangladeshis who lost their homes in the 2020 floods were financially well off enough that they were able to get bank loans to rebuild. Being dirt poor, however, Salma and her husband and four children ended up destitute. They had no choice but to move to one of the sprawling slums in the country's capital, Dhaka, the population of which now exceeds 20 million.

> ## CONSIDER THIS
>
> A 2022 study estimated that floods in the United States, including the ones that strike neighborhoods dominated by people of color, did $32 billion worth of damages.
>
> —*Nature Climate Change*

Effects on the Elderly

A certain percentage of poorer folk in every society are elderly. But whether they are of meager financial means or well-to-do, people older than fifty-five have higher risks of suffering from various ill effects of climate change. Heat waves, for example, pose such a risk. But in the bigger communities—especially in large cities like Dhaka, India's Calcutta, Mexico City, Chicago, and Los Angeles—the adverse effects of those heat events can be magnified. The phenomenon in question is called the urban heat island effect, and it occurs when streets, sidewalks, and other paved surfaces absorb sunlight and radiate that stored heat back into the air, causing higher environmental temperatures.

Older city dwellers who are fortunate enough to have air conditioners in their homes are less likely to feel the strain of the urban heat island effect. The problem, experts say, is that the elderly who do not have that luxury often are less mobile than younger people. Therefore, says Gregory Wellenius of the Boston University School of Public Health, the elderly "find it hard to move to cooling centers, which is a challenge."[32]

Another way that climate change can harm elderly people is by heightening the severity of respiratory illnesses. First, climate change causes droughts, which frequently increase the amount of dust particles in the air. Similarly, the giant wildfires that are increasingly driven by the warming climate send clouds of toxic

Climate Change and Indigenous Peoples

According to the United Nations Development Programme, in 2023 there were roughly 370 million indigenous people in the world. Indigenous, or native, people are the earliest-known inhabitants of a region, especially a region that was later colonized by a now-dominant group. Summarizing the United Nation's recent studies of the effects of climate change on those peoples, Turkish reporters Yeter Ada Seko and Emre Basaran report that native peoples

are among the worst-hit due to rising temperatures, and their effects. [Those effects] include epidemics, drought, desertification, forest fires, deforestation, heavy rains that can damage agriculture, river floods, and the melting of glaciers. . . . As a result, local indigenous peoples have lost their livelihoods, while being exposed to food insecurity and invasive new insect species due to temperature changes.... For instance, in the Equatorial Amazon, climate change–induced excessive rainfall has led to devastating floods in agricultural lands, impacting the main source of income for local communities and causing food security concerns. [Meanwhile] in Australia, the Aborigines . . . already face irregular tides, coastal erosion, rising water levels, and flash flooding.

Yeter Ada Seko and Emre Basaran, "Indigenous Peoples' Ways of Life Threatened by Climate Change," Anadolu Agency, July 14, 2023. www.aa.com.

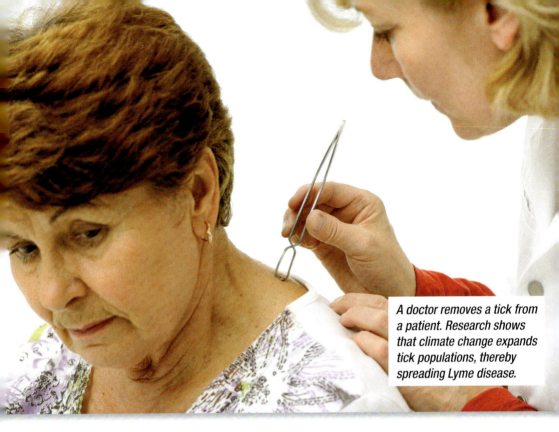

A doctor removes a tick from a patient. Research shows that climate change expands tick populations, thereby spreading Lyme disease.

smoke into communities near and far. These and other forms of air pollution that climate change either causes or makes worse regularly increase the incidence of illness among older adults.

One more way the climate crisis increases health risks for elderly folk is tied directly to the warming of the planet's atmosphere. In recent years that extra warmth has steadily expanded the habitable range of ticks. That has put people of all ages in affected areas at greater risk of contracting Lyme disease, which many ticks carry. But numerous studies show that individuals aged fifty-five to sixty-nine are far more liable to contract that illness than younger people.

Climate Change and People of Color

People of color are another large societal group that is unusually vulnerable to the effects of climate change. A 2021 report by the EPA showed that African Americans, for example, are 40 percent more likely to live in less affluent sections of the larger cities,

CONSIDER THIS

Large storms, wildfires, and other extreme climate change–driven events can cause some children to experience anxiety and other mental health conditions.

—US Environmental Protection Agency

and those are the areas that experience the highest rates of heat-related deaths during heat waves.

Other studies have indicated similar types of problems in several sectors of the American South. In coastal communities both large and small, African Americans make up a hefty proportion of the local populations. Also, the areas in which most of them live tend to be low-lying and highly prone to flooding from both sea level rise and large hurricanes.

Furthermore, major research published in 2022 in the scientific journal *Nature Climate Change* suggests that this disadvantage will get progressively worse in the next few decades. The study found that the regions of coastal communities in which Blacks and Latinos predominate will have far higher risks of destructive floods as the earth's atmosphere gets hotter. And those risks will not be restricted to physical injury and death. They will also in-

Negative Effects on Pregnant Women and Children

According to a study conducted by the United Nations, the results of which were reported in November 2023, pregnant women, babies, and small children face serious health risks from disasters caused or worsened by climate change. The year 2023, the report says, was particularly marked by a series of devastating wildfires, floods, heat waves, and droughts. These calamities have displaced huge numbers of people, killed crops and livestock, and made air pollution worse than ever. In addition, the study found that climate change has been speeding up the spread of debilitating and deadly diseases, including dengue fever, cholera, and malaria. All of these diseases can have devastating consequences for pregnant women and children who contract them. The study also cites research that shows that the negative effects of climate change can begin even in the womb. In such cases the results can be pregnancy-related complications such as preterm birth, low birth weight, and stillbirth. For those children who survive, the damage caused can last a lifetime, affecting the development of both their body and brain as they grow.

This Aboriginal family stands in front of their hut. Australia's Aboriginal people are at high risk for danger brought on by climate change because they frequently live in areas that experience severe heat-related weather.

clude financial damages in the billions of dollars, much of which insurance companies will not cover.

Kristen Broady, who works at the Brookings Institution, an organization that studies economics and other social sciences, has researched the roots of these inequities. She points out that it is no accident that people of color often live in areas that are prone to the harsher effects of natural disasters. Much of it, she says, is concerned with how land used to be, and in some places still is, valued. "When you assess land's value," she asks, "is it in a flood plain, or near a power plant? . . . And who could afford to live there? That gets to income, and once you get to income we would see that African American and Latino or Hispanic people, on average, earn less."[33] Hence, Broady emphasizes, often the only land parcels people in those groups can afford to buy are the ones that have higher risks of flooding.

Help from the Community as a Whole

Poor people, individuals with disabilities, the elderly, and people of color are far from the only societal groups that are particularly vulnerable to the adverse ramifications of climate change. For instance, young children tend to be more vulnerable than adults to the ill effects of heat waves, floods and wildfires that lead to homelessness and tick infestations. Likewise, air pollution, dirty water, and abnormally high temperatures—all increasingly driven by climate change—can cause pregnant women to miscarry or give birth to premature or stillborn babies. And members of indigenous populations, such as Native Americans in the United States and the Aboriginal people in Australia, are also at high risk for climate change effects. This is because they frequently dwell in areas where severe storms, drought, desertification, wildfires, and deforestation are common.

Each of these groups in a community has its own reasons for being more susceptible to certain aspects of climate change. The overriding question, asks Tahseen Jafry, a climate expert at Scotland's Glasgow Caledonian University, is whether the larger community is obligated to help them. Indeed, she argues, regarding the onrush of climate change, the most vulnerable among us are sometimes at a disadvantage and need a helping hand. And those in society who can lend that hand should do so. "There's no doubt in my mind," she states, "that we have a moral obligation to support and to give back where we can so that we are protecting humanity."[34]

CHAPTER FIVE

Communities Adapting to Climate Change

Every year tens of thousands of tourists from around the globe flock to Belize, a tiny Central American nation nestled between the Caribbean Sea to the east and Guatemala to the west. Attracted by year-round sunshine, magnificent beaches, and vibrant coral reefs, the visitors stay at luxury hotels equipped with all the modern amenities. Sadly, a great many of those visitors are unaware of the living conditions in many of the communities lying outside Belize's tourist hot spots. Located in or near the country's tropical forests, the more rural hamlets lack several of the comforts that people in the United States see as basic and take for granted. Several of Belize's small towns have no electricity, for example. This is because the nation has a very small electrical grid, and a lot of the rural communities cannot afford to hook up to it.

That regrettable situation is steadily improving, however. A pickup truck loaded with solar panels now frequents the dusty roads that pass by towering stone temples erected centuries ago by the Mayans. The vehicle carries three descendants of those ancient people—Florentina Choco, Miriam Choc, and Cristina Choc. Born in a poor rural village, as adults they became determined to bring electrical power to their community. Eventually, they heard about the Global Environment Facility (GEF), a UN-sponsored program dedicated to helping poorer nations protect the environment. GEF paid for the three women to take courses offered by Barefoot College International. The latter organization operates regional centers that train rural women in poor nations to become solar engineers.

After earning their certificates in that high-tech profession, these graduates began installing solar energy systems in small communities in Belize's southern province of Toledo. "These women are shattering the glass ceiling!" remarks Leonel Requena, a local coordinator for GEF. "They have installed solar systems to four indigenous communities impacting over 1,000 residents."[35] In one of those villages—Graham Creek—Requena points out, Choco, Choc, and Choc installed sun-powered systems in some twenty-five homes, which brought electricity to more than 150 people. The three women also installed solar panels in a local school attended by thirty children.

> **CONSIDER THIS**
>
> At least 500 million people worldwide live in communities that lack electricity.
>
> —United Nations

When they first began studying solar energy, the three women did not anticipate that they would be doing more than supplying electricity to residents who needed it. But in time they learned that they would also be making a small reduction in the global threat of climate change. Some of the experts on the UN's GEF team were curious about just how big that reduction was. So in early 2022 they did the math and found that the three women's recent, modest solar power installations had already removed 14,330 pounds (6.5 metric tons) of carbon dioxide and other greenhouse gases from the atmosphere. Impressed, Requena told some media reporters, "Women are outstanding leaders in Belize, driving the sustainable development agenda [that fosters] harmony between nature and people for the benefit of both."[36]

Learning to Adapt to the Climate Threat

Of course, the three solar engineers had no illusions about the planetary impact of their efforts. And neither did the members of

Children play in the Mayan community of San Miguel in Toledo, Belize. Solar panels were recently installed in a number of villages in this region as a way to supply electricity to residents who need it.

the GEF team who sponsored them. Each year humanity releases some 14 trillion pounds (6.4 billion metric tons) of greenhouse gases into the air. So clearly, on a global level the dent the women had made in the vast accumulation of those gases was in a sense microscopic.

Yet efforts like those of Choco and her colleagues remain important in a different way. Their harnessing of solar power for the good of communities on the local level is less about fighting climate change and more about adapting to it. As the atmosphere has grown warmer in recent years, Belize has experienced more heat waves than ever before. And a side effect of that trend is longer stretches of sunny days. In turn, that makes solar panels more reliable and cost effective as power sources there, a fact that the three Mayan women have taken full advantage of.

Many communities worldwide, small and large alike, are coming to accept an unfortunate but self-evident reality. Namely, the warming of the atmosphere and oceans over the course of the past two or so centuries has already caused certain climatic changes that cannot be reversed. So even if humans eventually do manage to slow down or halt the onrush of climate change, the atmosphere's average overall temperature will never go back to its pre-1900 level. As a result of such irreversible changes, says Pulitzer Prize–winning journalist Elizabeth Kolbert, "billions of people will have to drastically change the way they live."[37] In the process, they will need to do their best to adapt in diverse ways to varying aspects of climate change.

Adapting to Extreme Weather Events

One of the most damaging of those aspects is the periodic onset of various kinds of extreme weather events, including heat waves, droughts, and bigger, more catastrophic storms. Although people cannot stop those events from happening, they can try to adapt to them by finding ways to lessen their severity.

Notable examples of that approach are recent efforts in several large American cities to reduce the urban heat island effect that makes the hottest days feel even hotter. Experts at the EPA and other environmental organizations now regularly recommend a series of so-called cooling strategies. One is to

Agricultural Adaptation to Climate Change

Protecting farmland, crops, and other food-producing resources and making them more efficient is one way that some countries and communities are adapting to the warming climate. One of the most notable examples is a program called the European Green Deal. The European Union (EU), an economic alliance of most of Europe's nations, approved the program in 2020. Its main goal is to make Europe's agricultural system totally sustainable and highly productive even as the climate grows warmer in the decades ahead. To achieve this formidable aim, the nations of the EU have set several smaller, targeted agricultural goals. One is to improve the quality of Europe's soils so that each square meter of farmland produces more food than it did in the past. Other goals include using advances in genetic engineering to make crops more pest resistant without resorting to toxic chemicals, and reducing food waste. Before 2020 Europeans wasted an estimated 130 trillion pounds (59 billion metric tons) of food each year.

Volunteers in Harlem, New York, paint a school roof with light-colored reflective paint, which has been found to lower building temperatures and reduce the need for air-conditioning.

increase the number of trees and large bushes in such a community. That not only provides extra shade but also reduces the amount of carbon dioxide in the air (through photosynthesis, in which green plants absorb that gas and release oxygen as a by-product).

Similarly, community residents are urged to grow plants of various kinds on the rooftops of large buildings when possible. Sometimes called "eco-roofs," these reduce the temperature of roof surfaces. This approach has been used extensively in Austin, Texas, as part of its 2020 environmental initiative designed to adapt to the warming climate.

Another way to cool down a city rooftop is to cover it with materials that reflect sunlight and heat away from the structure. A bonus is that this approach also decreases the quantity of energy needed to keep the building's interior cooler. Both the city-state of Singapore in Southeast Asia and New York City have had considerable success with this approach. According to journalist Pablo Robles and his colleagues:

> Singapore has painted the roofs of some buildings with light-colored reflective paints, which absorb less heat and could reduce the ambient temperature around the buildings by up to 3.5 degrees Fahrenheit. . . . A similar program in New York City has covered more than 10 million square feet of rooftops with reflective paints since 2009, reducing the need for air conditioning and the waste heat it generates.[38]

Protecting Vital Fresh Water Sources

Other ongoing efforts to adapt to the steadily warming climate are those in which communities focus on protecting farmlands and the supplies of fresh water needed to sustain them. One of the more remarkable projects designed to protect existing vital water sources has been taking place in the South American nation of Colombia. There in 2020 an alliance of communities located to the northeast of the country's capital, Bogota, launched a program called Guardianas de los Páramos (or Páramos Women Guardians).

The goal of the project is to adapt to the warming climate by protecting the páramos ecosystems. These ecosystems, which consist of thick-leafed bushes and wide-bladed grasses, are found only in the highlands of the Andes Mountain range in Ecuador, Peru, Colombia, and Venezuela. Colombia has more than half of the existing páramos. Normally, warm air from nearby lowlands mixes with colder air from the mountain heights. This produces a great deal of rain, which soaks into the mountain soils and gives

---

CONSIDER THIS

In recent years the Colombian city of Medellín planted more than 880,000 trees around the urban area, reducing the average air temperature in the area by 8°F (4.5°C).

—*New York Times*

The páramos ecosystems, which consist of thick-leafed bushes and wide-bladed grasses (pictured), supply Colombia with 85 percent of the fresh water it uses for agriculture, as well as for drinking and bathing.

rise to the sponge-like plants in the páramos ecosystems. Those systems presently supply Colombia with 85 percent of the fresh water it uses for agriculture, as well as for drinking and bathing.

The current problem, a spokesperson for the UN explains, is that "the increase in temperatures and changes in rain patterns due to climate change poses a threat to these ecosystems."[39] Hoping to adapt to those changes, he continues, the communities that maintain the existing ecosystems use sophisticated sensors to keep a close watch on the plant life within them. This produces ongoing data about how rainfall patterns in the Andes are changing as a result of the warming climate. The hope is that over time the data will allow the experts to devise adaptation strategies that will save most, if not all, of the páramos ecosystems.

Adapting to the Encroaching Oceans

Still another aspect of climate change that many communities worldwide are now forced to adapt to is sea level rise. Fourteen of the world's seventeen largest cities lie on ocean coastlines.

Helping Communities' Most Vulnerable Members

In some countries, certain communities are adapting to climate change by helping those in society who are most vulnerable to the effects of the warming planet. An outstanding example is an ongoing program in the southern Venezuelan province of Amazonas. There, in the tropical rain forests, several local indigenous tribes have been displaced from their communities in part because of environmental and economic troubles stemming from climate change. Among those native peoples are the Panare, Bari, Guajibo, and Yanomami. Sponsored by the Global Environment Facility (GEF), the new program, dubbed Amazonas Originaria, is resettling the displaced people in a neighboring forest. The program is also training the tribespeople how to manage farms that grow a range of profitable crops, including cocoa. About the program, one of GEF's officials, Alexis Bermudez, states, "This project, in particular, is interesting and inspiring, as it is led by women . . . and it supports the fight against climate change, since its purpose is to conserve the Amazon Forest as the main carbon sink in southern Venezuela, working hand in hand with native communities, valuing their traditions and protecting their ancestral habitat."

Quoted in United Nations, "Small Solutions, Big Impacts: 5 Community-Based Projects Tackling Climate Change," April 28, 2022. https://news.un.org.

And by 2023, more than half of the approximately 640 million residents of those coastal communities were already feeling measurable damaging effects of the encroaching oceans. Moreover, numerous smaller cities and towns located on coastlines around the globe began to experience flooding events caused by rising sea levels in the early 2020s. Climate scientists have measured the present rate of sea level rise and predict that by 2050 at the latest, more than 800 million residents of the world's coastal communities will be threatened with frequent, severe flooding.

Among the first of the larger coastal cities to experience such flooding on a regular basis was Miami, Florida. In the two decades preceding 2020, incidences of flooding caused by sea level rise increased by an incredible 320 percent. Out of necessity, local leaders have instituted measures designed to help the city steadily adapt to the changing climate.

One of the more innovative and effective of these strategies was the creation in May 2021 of an anti–climate change office for Miami and its surrounding county. Jane Gilbert, a city-planning strategist with thirty years of experience, was appointed to head the new department. Her aggressive actions, including the construction of a complex array of seawalls to hold back the rising ocean waters, have set a standard for other coastal cities worldwide to follow.

> ## CONSIDER THIS
>
> The US Army Corps of Engineers is considering erecting a seawall 6 miles (9.7 km) long and 20 feet (6.1 m) high around parts of the city of Miami, Florida.
>
> —*New York Times*

A Two-Pronged Approach

Although these and other examples of adaptation to climate change are important, all the experts point out that by itself adaptation is not enough. Equally important, they point out, is mitigation, or fighting against and slowing down the rate and severity of climate change. That, they say, can only be accomplished by serious reductions in the amount of greenhouse gases humanity pumps into the atmosphere.

Thus, communities everywhere need to take a two-pronged approach to the warming climate—a healthy mix of mitigation and adaptation. As the scientists at the prestigious University Corporation for Atmospheric Research, in Boulder, Colorado, put it, "To survive and thrive, we need to adapt as the climate changes and also limit the amount of warming by reducing greenhouse gases. . . . The more we can mitigate climate change to reduce the amount of warming, the less we will need to adapt. However, both mitigation and adaptation are necessary as we respond to climate change."[40]

SOURCE NOTES

Introduction: Communities Threatened by a Warming World

1. Ezra David Romero, "San Francisco's Aging Infrastructure Isn't Ready for Its Wetter Future," KQED, July 8, 2023. www.kqed.org.
2. Quoted in Romero, "San Francisco's Aging Infrastructure Isn't Ready for Its Wetter Future."
3. Moody's Analytics, "The Impact of Climate Change on U.S. Subnational Economies," February 1, 2023. www.moodysanalytics.com.
4. State of California, "California's Fourth Climate Change Assessment," August 28, 2018. www.energy.ca.gov.
5. Allegra Kirkland et al., "What Climate Change Will Do to Three Major American Cities by 2100," Quartz, October 18, 2019. https://qz.com.
6. Moody's Analytics, "The Impact of Climate Change on U.S. Subnational Economies."
7. Quoted in Kirkland et al., "What Climate Change Will Do to Three Major American Cities by 2100."

Chapter One: Destruction Caused by Extreme Weather

8. American Geophysical Union, "New Study Finds Most Communities Will Encounter Heavy Rainfall, Excessive Heat Under Climate Change," September 14, 2023. https://phys.org.
9. Quoted in American Geophysical Union, "New Study Finds Most Communities Will Encounter Heavy Rainfall, Excessive Heat Under Climate Change."
10. Oliver Milman, "Hottest Ocean Temperatures in History Recorded Last Year," *The Guardian* (Manchester, UK), January 11, 2022. www.theguardian.com.
11. Union of Concerned Scientists, "Hurricanes and Climate Change," June 25, 2019. www.ucsusa.org.
12. Daniel Bedford and John Cook, *Climate Change: Examining the Facts*. Santa Barbara, CA: ABC-CLIO, 2017, p. xiv.
13. Quoted in Bedford and Cook, *Climate Change*, p. 144.

Chapter Two: Threats to Fresh Water and Food Production

14. Quoted in Al Jazeera, "Somalia Faces Worst Famine in Half a Century, UN Warns," News24, October 19, 2022. www.news24.com.

15. Quoted in World Food Programme, "Act Now on Climate Crisis or Millions More Will Be Pushed into Hunger and Famine," November 18, 2021. www.wfp.org.
16. Tulane University School of Public Health & Tropical Medicine, "5 Things to Know About the Saltwater Intrusion of the Mississippi River," September 28, 2023. https://sph.tulane.edu.
17. Quoted in Sara Jerving, "Livestock Dies in Droves in Somalia, and Without Rains 'Humans Are Next,'" Devex, March 16, 2022. https://devex.shorthandstories.com.
18. International Rescue Committee, "Crisis in Somalia: Catastrophic Hunger Amid Drought and Conflict," March 20, 2023. www.rescue.org.
19. Climate Reality Project, "How the Climate Crisis Is Impacting Bangladesh," December 9, 2021. www.climaterealityproject.org.
20. Quoted in US Embassy and Consulates in Italy, "How Climate Change Affects the Food Crisis," October 16, 2022. https://it.usembassy.gov.
21. Quoted in US Embassy and Consulates in Italy, "How Climate Change Affects the Food Crisis."

Chapter Three: Residents of Communities Displaced

22. Abrahm Lustgarten, "The Great Climate Migration," *New York Times*, July 23, 2020. www.nytimes.com.
23. Lustgarten, "The Great Climate Migration."
24. Jonathan Blazer and Katie Hoeppner, "Five Things to Know About the Right to Seek Asylum," September 29, 2022. www.aclu.org.
25. Lustgarten, "The Great Climate Migration."
26. Lustgarten, "The Great Climate Migration."

Chapter Four: Climate Change's Impact on the Most Vulnerable

27. Quoted in Climate Reality Project, "Disability and Climate Crisis," April 19, 2021. www.climaterealityproject.org.
28. Quoted in Climate Reality Project, "Disability and Climate Crisis."
29. US Environmental Protection Agency, "Climate Change and the Health of People with Disabilities," December 13, 2022. www.epa.org.
30. World Economic Forum, "The Climate Crisis Disproportionately Hits the Poor. How Can We Protect Them?," January 13, 2023. www.weforum.org.

31. Quoted in France 24, "Bangladesh's Shantytowns for Climate Refugees," October 26, 2021. www.france24.com.
32. Quoted in Oliver Milman, "'Silent Killer': Experts Warn of Record US Deaths from Extreme Heat," *The Guardian* (Manchester, UK), August 1, 2023. www.theguardian.com.
33. Quoted in Patrick Gayley, "Black Neighborhoods at Risk as Climate Change Accelerates Flooding," NBC News, January 31, 2022. www.nbcnews.com.
34. Quoted in Environmental Justice Foundation, "No Shelter from the Storm: The Urgent Need to Recognize and Protect Climate Refugees," June 1, 2021. https://ejfoundation.org.

Chapter Five: Communities Adapting to Climate Change

35. Quoted in United Nations, "Small Solutions, Big Impacts: 5 Community-Based Projects Tackling Climate Change," April 28, 2022. https://news.un.org.
36. Quoted in United Nations, "Small Solutions, Big Impacts."
37. Quoted in David Remnick and Henry Finder, *The Fragile Earth: Writing from the* New Yorker *on Climate Change*. New York: Ecco, 2020, p. 534.
38. Pablo Robles et al., "How to Cool Down a City," *New York Times*, September 18, 2023. www.nytimes.com.
39. United Nations, "Small Solutions, Big Impacts."
40. University Corporation for Atmospheric Research, "Adapting to Climate Change," 2023. https://scied.ucar.edu.

ORGANIZATIONS AND WEBSITES

Center for Climate and Energy Solutions (C2ES)
www.c2es.org
C2ES, formerly called the Pew Center on Global Climate Change, promotes reducing carbon dioxide emissions and adopting cleaner energy solutions. The website features links to information on how both individuals and groups can support C2ES and thereby help fight climate change.

Intergovernmental Panel on Climate Change (IPCC)
www.ipcc.ch
The IPCC is the leading international organization presently studying and fighting climate change. Its website provides up-to-date reports on the activities of several IPCC working groups, plus tells how students and other everyday people can get involved in efforts to stop climate change.

National Oceanic and Atmospheric Administration (NOAA)
www.noaa.gov
NOAA's main website provides a simple definition for climate change, along with links to helpful articles on the subject. There are also links to climate predictions by scientists and information from the National Weather Service.

US Global Change Research Program
www.globalchange.gov
This federal agency examines the impact of climate change on the planet and society. Its website offers many reports, webinars, podcasts, videos, and other resources that review in detail the concerns related to specific environmental threats.

World Meteorological Organization (WMO)
https://wmo.int
The WMO's website has many links to articles relating to global weather patterns and how they affect human civilization. Visitors to the site will find links to helpful publications about climate change, and a "WMO for Youth" section provides entertaining activities related to fighting climate change.

FOR FURTHER RESEARCH

Books

Lynn H. Cooper, *Climate Change*. Chicago: Readzone, 2023.

Bill Gates, *How to Avoid a Climate Disaster*. Vancouver, WA: Vintage, 2022.

Joanne Mattern, *Wildfires*. Minnetonka, MN: Kaleidoscope, 2023.

Olsin McGann, *A Short, Hopeful Guide to Climate Change*. Dublin, Ireland: Little Island, 2022.

Andrea Minoglio and Laura Fanelli, *Our World Out of Balance: Understanding Climate Change*. San Francisco: Blue Dot Kids, 2020.

Carla Mooney, *Climate in Crisis*. Norwich, VT: Nomad, 2022.

Internet Sources

Brodie Boland et al., "How Cities Can Adapt to Climate Change," McKinsey Sustainability, July 20, 2021. www.mckinsey.com.

Imperial College London, "What Are the Impacts of Climate Change?," 2023. www.imperial.ac.uk.

International Research Group for Science and Society, "Adapting Agriculture to Climate Today, for Tomorrow." https://iri.columbia.edu.

Jared Mendenhall, "Wildfire's Impact on Our Environment," Utah Department of Environmental Quality. July 27, 2023. https://deq.utah.gov.

Emma Pattee, "How to Prepare for Climate Change's Most Immediate Impacts," *Wired*, January 16, 2022. www.wired.com.

United Nations, "Small Solutions, Big Impacts: 5 Community-Based Projects Tackling Climate Change," April 28, 2022. https://news.un.org.

Greg Wong, "SF Must Update Infrastructure for Extreme Heat, Reports Found," *San Francisco Examiner*, July 19, 2023. www.sfexaminer.com.

World Bank, "Social Dimensions of Climate Change," 2023. www.worldbank.org.

World Economic Forum, "The Climate Crisis Disproportionately Hits the Poor. How Can We Protect Them?," January 13, 2023. www.weforum.org.

World Health Organization, "Climate Change Is an Urgent Threat to Pregnant Women and Children," November 21, 2023. www.who.int.

INDEX

Note: Boldface page numbers indicate illustrations.

Aborigines, 42, **45**
Africa
    food insecurity in, 15, 18–19
    growth of Sahara Desert in, 31
    increase in rainfall in, 24
See also specific nations
African Americans, 43–45
age and heat waves, 41–43, **43**
agriculture
    difficulties for farmers in normally wet-
        hot regions getting wetter and hotter,
        24–27
    effects of climate change on, in
        Guatemala, 28–29
    European Green Deal, 50
    flooding and, 24, 25
    rainfall and, 25, 28, 42
    sea level rise and, 26–27, 40–41
    in Somalia, 23–24
    See also food insecurity
Alaska, 34
Amazonas Originaria, 54
Amazon rain forests, 42, 54
American Civil Liberties Union, 32
American Geophysical Union, 9
aquifers, 21
Australia, 16, **16**, 42, **45**

Bangladesh, **26**
    climate migrants from, **33**
    percentage of population living below
        poverty line, 41
    sea level rise and loss of land for
        agriculture in, 26–27, 40–41
Barefoot College International, 48
Bari people, 54
Basaran, Emre, 42
Bedford, Daniel, 17
Belize, 47–49, **49**
Bermudez, Alexis, 54
Biden, Joe, 27, 34
Blinken, Antony, 27
Broady, Kristen, 45

Brookings Institution, 45

California
    Death Valley temperatures, 15
    San Joaquin Valley food production, 25
    wildfires in, 17
California Energy Commission, 5
Canada, wildfires in, 17
Caribbean Islands
    Belize, 47–49, **49**
    climate migrants from, 28–29, **30**
Center for Climate and Energy Solutions,
    16
Centers for Disease Control and
    Prevention, 39
Charles, Dan, 21
children
    food insecurity and death, 18, 24
    Guatemalan, suffering from food
        insecurity, 29
    mental health conditions and extreme
        weather, 44
China, flash flooding in, 11
Choc, Cristina, 47–48
Choc, Miriam, 47–48
Choco, Florentina, 47–48
climate change
    basic facts about, 5
    costs of, to governments and large
        companies, 9
    as existential issue for humanity, 14
    language for effects of, 4
    US communities most at risk due to,
        4, **6**
climate (in)equity, described, 39–40
climate migrants, **30**
    from Amazon rain forests, 54
    from Americas and Caribbean Islands,
        28–29, **30**
    from Bangladesh, **33**
    described, 28–29
    food insecurity and, 34
    from Guatemala, 28–29, **30**
    internal, described, 35, 41
    from Pacific Ocean island nations,
        35–37, **36**

61

projection of future, 31
  Native American Indian nations, 32, 34
  number of people displaced by 2050, 29, 30
  rights of, 21
  from Southeast Asia, **33**, 33–35
  US as destination of, 31–33
Climate Reality Project, 27
Colombia, 52–53, **53**
Cook, John, 17
cooling strategies, 50–52, **51**
costs of climate change, 9, 12–13, **13**
  See also deaths
Cyclone Sitrang, 26

deaths
  of children and food insecurity, 18, 24
  from Cyclone Sitrang, 26
  from flash flooding, 11, 25, 35
  from heat waves, 44
  during hurricanes, 6, 13
disasters, recovery from, 7
diseases, spread of, 43, **43**, 44
Djordjevic, Slobodan, 11
droughts
  dust particles in air and, 42
  food insecurity and, 22–23, **23**
  groundwater, 21
  prolonged, and food insecurity, 15
  supplies of fresh, usable water and, 20

Earth's Future (journal), 8
eco-roofs, 51
ecosystems, rainfall and, 52–53
Elder, James, 18
electricity, 48
Environmental Justice Foundation, 35
European Green Deal, 50
European Union (EU), 50

flooding, flash
  agriculture and, 24, 25
  in Bangladesh, **26**
  in China, 11
  deaths from, 11, 25, 35
  in New York City, 10, 11
  rainfall events and, 10, 11
  in San Francisco, 5
Florence (Hurricane), 12
Florida
  hurricanes in, 13, **13**

insurers' abandonment of, 7
  rise in sea level and saltwater intrusions into groundwater in, 22
food insecurity, **20**
  climate migrants and, 34
  death of children and, 18, 24
  droughts and, 15, 22–23, **23**
  Guatemalan children suffering from, 29
  military conflicts and, 19
  in normally wet-hot regions getting wetter and hotter, 24–27
food waste, 50

Gilbert, Jane, 55
Global Environment Facility (GEF), 47–48, 54
greenhouse gases
  release of, 5, 40
  solar energy and, 48
Guajibo people, 54
Guardian, The (newspaper), 26
Guardianas de los Páramos (or Páramos Women Guardians), 52–53, **53**
Guatemala, 28–29, **30**

Hassan, Hawa, 23–24
Hayhoe, Katharine, 7
heat waves
  absorption of rainfall and, 9
  age and, 41–43, **43**
  areas with highest number of deaths from, 44
  during summer of 2023, 14
  wildfires and, 16
Hispanic people, 44–45
hurricanes, monster
  costs of, 12–13, **13**
  deaths from, 13
  Ida in Louisiana, 11–12
  ocean temperatures and, 12

Ian (Hurricane), 13, **13**
Ida (Hurricane), 11–12
indigenous peoples
  Aborigines, 42, **45**
  in Amazon rain forests, 42, 54
  in Belize, 47–49, **49**
  in Equatorial Amazon, 42
  Native American communities threatened by rising sea levels, 32, 34

individuals with disabilities and extreme weather, 38–39, **40**
Institute for Economics and Peace, 30
International Rescue Committee, 20, 24

Kiribati, **36**, 36–37
Kirkland, Allegra, 6
Kolbert, Elizabeth, 50

Laganda, Gernot, 19
Lake Chad (Africa), 15
language, for effects of climate change, 4
Latinos, 44–45
Louisiana, 11–12, 22
Lustgarten, Abrahm, 29, 35, 37
Lyme disease, 43, **43**

malnutrition. *See* food insecurity
May, Kris, 4
Medellin, Colombia, 52
Miami, Florida, and rising sea level, 9, **10**, 54–55
military conflicts, 19
Milman, Oliver, 12
Moody's Analytics, 4, 7

National Interagency Fire Center, 17
National Weather Service, 15
Nature Climate Change (journal), 15, 41, 44–45
New Orleans, hurricanes, 11–12
New York City
    Hurricane Ida, 12
    rainfall and flash flooding in, 10, 11
    rising sea level and, 9
    roofs with reflective paint, **51**, 51–52
New York Times (newspaper), 9, 32, 52, 55
Nigeria, 25

oceans, 12, 19
    See also sea level, rise in

Pacific Ocean island nations, annihilation of, 35–37, **36**
Panare people, 54
people of color, 43–45
Phoenix, Arizona, 14
power outages, in San Francisco, 5–6
predictions
    about climate migrants, 29, 30, 31
    about coastal flooding (by 2050), 54

disappearance of Pacific Island nations, 35–37, **36**
increase in temperatures in future, 30–31
Native American communities threatened, 32, 34
pregnant women, 44
Proceedings of the National Academy of Sciences, 30

Quartz (website), 6
Quinault Indian Nation, 32, 34

rainfall
    agricultural production and, 25, 28, 42
    ecosystems and, 52–53
    flooding from, 10, 11
    heat waves and absorption of, 9
    increase in, in Africa, 24
    increase in atmospheric moisture and, 8
    monster hurricanes, 11–13, **13**
    saltwater intrusion and lack of, 22
    wildfires and, 21
Requena, Leonel, 48
respiratory illnesses, 42–43
Robles, Pablo, 52
Romero, Ezra David, 4
Romm, Joseph, 14

Sahara Desert, growth of, 31
Sally (Hurricane), 13
Salma, Bibi, 41
saltwater intrusions into fresh water, 21–22
San Francisco, 4, 5–6, **6**
Schmucker, Rachel, 38–39
sea level, rise in
    annihilation of Pacific Ocean island nations, 35–37, **36**
    loss of land for agriculture and, 26–27, 40–41
    Miami and, 9, 54–55
    New York City and, 9
    prediction about coastal flooding (by 2050), 54
    saltwater intrusions into groundwater and, 22
    San Francisco and, 5
    world's largest cities and, 53–54
Seko, Yeter Ada, 42
Singapore, 51–52

63

solar energy, 47–49
Somalia, 18–19, **20**, 23–24
Southeast Asian climate migrants, **33**, 33–35
South Sudan, 18, 19

Tahseen Jafry, 46
Texas, **22**
trees, planting of, 51, 52
Trenberth, Kevin, 17

United Nations Development Programme, 42
United States
  as destination of climate migrants, 31–33
  heat-related hospitalizations in, 39
  Native American communities threatened by rising sea levels, 32, 34
  number of Americans living within 3 miles of large-scale wildfires, 17
  wildfires in, 16
  See also New York City; specific states
University Corporation for Atmospheric Research, 55
urban heat island effect, 41–42
US Army Corps of Engineers, 22, 55
US Environmental Protection Agency (EPA)
  cooling strategies, 50–52, **51**
  extreme weather effects on children, 44
  extreme weather risks for individuals with disabilities, 39
  extreme weather risks for people of color, 43–44

Venezuela, 54

Washington State, 32
water
  aquifers, 21
  monster hurricanes, 11–13, **13**
  páramos ecosystem in Colombia, 52–53, **53**
  usable,
    assumption of existence of, 19
      availability of, 6
      groundwater drought and, 21

    saltwater intrusions and, 21–22
    temperature and ability of air to hold, 8–9
    wildfires and, 21
    See also rainfall
weather, extreme
  areas getting dry-hot
    conditions in, 13–14
    examples of, 14
    patterns beginning in Pacific Ocean, 19
    prolonged drought in, 15
    wildfires in, 15–17, **16**
  areas getting wet-hot
    difficulties for farmers in normally wet-hot regions, 24–27
    hurricanes and, 11–13, **13**
    location and population of, 9
    reasons for, 8
  children's mental health conditions and, 44
  effects on poor people and poorer nations, 40–41
  individuals with disabilities and, 38–39, **40**
Wellenius, Gregory, 42
wildfires, **16**
  areas most affected, 15–16
  heat waves and, 16
  number of Americans living within 3 miles of large-scale, 17
  rainfall and, 21
  toxic smoke from, 42–43
  usable water and, 21
women
  Amazonas Originaria resettlement of climate migrants and, 54
  Barefoot College International and solar energy, 48
  ecosystem protection efforts of, 52–53, **53**
  pregnant, 44
World Bank, 29, 33–34
World Economic Forum, 40
World Weather Attribution, 19
Wu, Haijiang, 8, 9

Yanomami people, 54

Zhengzhou, China, 11